just mom and me

just
mom
AND
me

**A Journal for
Mothers and Sons**

ROCKRIDGE
PRESS

Interior and Cover Designer: Patricia Fabricant
Art Producer: Janice Ackerman
Editor: Sean Newcott
Production Editor: Jax Berman
Production Manager: Jose Olivera

Illustrations: Courtesy of Shutterstock

Paperback ISBN: 978-1-63807-981-1
R0

THIS JOURNAL BELONGS TO:

....

MOM

and

....

SON

GETTING STARTED

What an exciting journey you're about to embark on! Journaling together will allow you to learn new things about each other by inspiring you to ask questions you might not have asked otherwise. This experience will bring you closer together.

This journal is an interactive way to capture your mother–son relationship. There's plenty of space to jot down your reflections every day. Short-answer prompts will reveal how each of you thinks while long-form questions offer opportunities for deeper conversation about topics relevant to both of you. Free-writing pages allow you to expand on your answers or talk about other issues important to you.

These prompts—some light and fun, others introspective and thought-provoking—will help you learn each other's hopes and dreams, share thoughts about the family and friends, and discover your special skills and talents. Get started on your year of journaling together by setting your expectations in the "Beginning the Year" section. Remember, you can start this journal whenever you want—anytime of the year is a great time to start! When you finish, the "Reflecting on the Year" section will allow for reflection on all you've learned about each other.

To get the most out of this journal:

Take your time. Don't feel you have to rush through a month's prompts at once. If you need more time during any section of the journal, just make sure your writing partner knows.

Listen without judging. You will be learning things about each other that you didn't know before, and you might have conflicting opinions. That's the beauty of journaling together. Keep an open mind and respect each other's differences.

Be honest. Don't feel like you have to hide anything or hold back. Journaling together is an opportunity for you to say everything you've ever wanted to say to each other. Let it all out.

Use kind words. You can be honest and still be respectful. Using kind words when you're writing about difficult subjects makes the message or concern easier to receive and understand.

Create a plan. If one of you is traveling, or you don't live together, you can pick the prompts you'll answer ahead of time and send them to each other via email or a letter. You can even text your answers. It could also be fun to use these prompts as inspiration for conversations during phone calls or video chats.

Make this journal your own. If the tips for using this journal don't work for you and your writing partner, do whatever will make the experience more meaningful. This is your journal and your experience. Have a good time on this journey!

BEGINNING THE YEAR

Before you start, set aside some time to sit down together and lay out your expectations for how you'll use this journal. You'll both be happier knowing where to fit journaling into your routines. Answer these questions honestly. Consider all of your obligations so you'll have realistic expectations of each other. Once you answer these questions, you'll be all set to jump in and get started!

WE STARTED THIS JOURNAL TOGETHER ON

A PICTURE OR PHOTO OF US AT THE BEGINNING OF THE YEAR

1. Why are we writing in this journal together?

....

....

....

2. When will we write in this journal? Will we do it every day?
   Once a week?

....

....

....

3. How much time do we need for each entry?

....

....

....

4. Should we plan time to talk afterward?

....

....

....

5. Will we go through the journal in order or skip around?

....

....

....

6. How will we decide which prompts to answer and when?

....

....

....

7. What could we do if we need more space to write?

....

....

....

8. What do we want to learn about each other by doing this journal?

....

....

....

MONTH ONE

....

The thing I love most about myself is:

....

....

You can tell when I'm in a silly mood because I:

....

....

If you want me to laugh like crazy, do this:

....

....

When I'm sad, I:

....

....

This week, I worried about:

....

....

mom

The thing I love most about myself is:

....

....

You can tell when I'm in a silly mood because I:

....

....

If you want me to laugh like crazy, do this:

....

....

When I'm sad, I:

....

....

This week, I worried about:

....

....

SON

What's something about you that you think I don't know?

....
....
....
....
....
....
....
....
....
....
....
....
....
....
....
....
....
....

mom

What's something about you that you think I don't know?

....
....
....
....
....
....
....
....
....
....
....
....
....
....
....
....
....
....
....

SON

Three things I want to know about you:

1. ....
2. ....
3. ....

My answers to the things you want to know about me:

....
....
....
....
....
....
....
....
....
....
....
....
....
....
....

mom

Three things I want to know about you:

1. ....

2. ....

3. ....

My answers to the things you want to know about me:

....

....

....

....

....

....

....

....

....

....

....

....

....

....

SON

This is something I'm really good at:

....

....

This is something I do well, but I don't like to do:

....

....

This is something I wish I had more time to do:

....

....

Two goals I have for this year are:

....

....

This is how I plan to achieve those goals:

....

....

mom

This is something I'm really good at:

....

....

This is something I do well, but I don't like to do:

....

....

This is something I wish I had more time to do:

....

....

Two goals I have for this year are:

....

....

This is how I plan to achieve those goals:

....

....

SON

Share what a day in your life is like.

....
....
....
....
....
....
....
....
....

What's your favorite way to spend downtime?

....
....
....
....
....
....
....
....
....

MOM

Share what a day in your life is like.

....
....
....
....
....
....
....
....

What's your favorite way to spend downtime?

....
....
....
....
....
....
....
....
....

SON

How did you feel when you learned you were going to have a son?

....
....
....
....
....
....
....
....
....
....
....
....
....
....
....
....
....
....
....
....

MOM

What was a decision I made as a mother that you didn't agree with? What would you have done instead?

....

....

....

....

....

....

....

....

....

....

....

....

....

....

....

....

SON

FREE WRITING SPACE

....

....

....

....

....

....

....

....

....

....

....

....

....

....

....

....

....

....

....

....

mom

FREE WRITING SPACE

....
....
....
....
....
....
....
....
....
....
....
....
....
....
....
....
....
....
....
....

SON

MONTH TWO

....

What's it really like to be an adult? What do you like, and what don't you like?

....

....

....

....

....

....

....

....

My thoughts on what you wrote about being a young boy:

....

....

....

....

....

....

....

....

MOM

What's it like being a young boy today? What do you like,
and what don't you like?

....

....

....

....

....

....

....

My thoughts on what you wrote about being an adult:

....

....

....

....

....

....

....

....

SON

If I could add one quality to our relationship, it would be
.... because:

....

....

If you could plan the perfect day for us, what would it look like?

....

....

....

The best thing that happened to me this week was:

....

....

My favorite mother-and-son pair in pop culture is
.... because:

....

....

....

MOM

If I could add one quality to our relationship, it would be

.... because:

....

....

If you could plan the perfect day for us, what would it look like?

....

....

....

The best thing that happened to me this week was:

....

....

My favorite mother-and-son pair in pop culture is

.... because:

....

....

....

SON

More money or more friends. Which would you choose? Why?

....
....
....
....
....
....
....
....

When I think about the future, I feel .... because:

....
....
....
....
....
....
....

mom

More money or more friends. Which would you choose? Why?

....
....
....
....
....
....
....
....

When I think about the future, I feel .... because:

....
....
....
....
....
....
....

SON

Share a secret talent that you have.

....
....
....
....
....
....
....
....

What's your favorite way to be creative?

....
....
....
....
....
....
....
....

MOM

Share a secret talent that you have.

....
....
....
....
....
....
....

What's your favorite way to be creative?

....
....
....
....
....
....
....
....

SON

One person in our family I wish I was closer to is
.... because:

....

....

....

....

....

....

....

....

....

....

....

....

....

....

....

....

....

....

mom

One person in our family I wish I was closer to is
....because:

....

....

....

....

....

....

....

....

....

....

....

....

....

....

....

....

....

SON

FREE WRITING SPACE

....
....
....
....
....
....
....
....
....
....
....
....
....
....
....
....
....
....
....
....
....
....

mom

FREE WRITING SPACE

....

....

....

....

....

....

....

....

....

....

....

....

....

....

....

....

....

....

....

SON

MONTH THREE

·····················

Right now, this is the thing I'm most focused on:

....

....

This is something that recently stressed me out:

....

....

Tell me about a good book you read or movie you saw
recently.

....

....

....

....

Tell me about something weird or interesting that you
recently learned about.

....

....

....

mom

Right now, this is the thing I'm most focused on:

....

....

This is something that recently stressed me out:

....

....

Tell me about a good book you read or movie you saw recently.

....

....

....

....

Tell me about something weird or interesting that you recently learned about.

....

....

....

SON

What's something important to you that you'd like me
to care about, too, and how can I be involved?

....

....

....

....

....

....

....

....

My thoughts on your response:

....

....

....

....

....

....

....

....

MOM

What's something important to you that you'd like me
to care about, too, and how can I be involved?

....
....
....
....
....
....
....

My thoughts on your response:

....
....
....
....
....
....
....
....

SON

Six things I tried and didn't like:

1. ....
2. ....
3. ....
4. ....
5. ....
6. ....

Six things I tried and liked:

1. ....
2. ....
3. ....
4. ....
5. ....
6. ....

mom

Six things I tried and didn't like:

1. ....
2. ....
3. ....
4. ....
5. ....
6. ....

Six things I tried and liked:

1. ....
2. ....
3. ....
4. ....
5. ....
6. ....

SON

If I didn't have work and other responsibilities, this is what I would do all day:

....

....

....

....

....

At your age, I thought adulthood would be:

....

....

....

....

These are the most surprising things about being an adult:

....

....

....

....

....

mom

If I didn't have school and other responsibilities, this is what I would do all day:

....
....
....
....
....

This is what I like the most about being young:

....
....
....
....

These are the ways growing up surprised me:

....
....
....
....
....

SON

Do you think of yourself as a dreamer? Why or why not?

MOM

Do you think of yourself as a dreamer? Why or why not?

....

....

....

....

....

....

....

....

....

....

....

....

....

....

....

....

....

....

SON

FREE WRITING SPACE

mom

FREE WRITING SPACE

MONTH FOUR

....

Tell me about a time when you put in extra effort and your hard work paid off. How did you feel?

....
....
....
....
....
....

When you were younger, what kind of job did you want? How is your work different from or similar to what you imagined as a child?

....
....
....
....
....
....
....
....
....
....

mom

Tell me about a time when you put in extra effort and your hard work paid off. How did you feel?

....

....

....

....

....

When you grow up, what kind of job do you want?
What kind of feeling do you want to get from your work?

....

....

....

....

....

....

....

....

SON

If you could be a kid forever or an adult forever, which would you choose and why?

....
....
....
....
....
....
....
....
....
....
....
....
....
....
....
....
....
....
....
....

MOM

If you could be a kid forever or an adult forever, which would you choose and why?

....

....

....

....

....

....

....

....

....

....

....

....

....

....

....

....

....

SON

Six things that make me special:

1. ....
2. ....
3. ....
4. ....
5. ....
6. ....

Six things that make you special:

1. ....
2. ....
3. ....
4. ....
5. ....
6. ....

mom

Six things that make me special:

1. ....
2. ....
3. ....
4. ....
5. ....
6. ....

Six things that make you special:

1. ....
2. ....
3. ....
4. ....
5. ....
6. ....

SON

This is the actress who would play me in a movie of our lives:

....

This is the actor who would play you in a movie of our lives:

....

I love when you and I do ....
together because:

....

....

The most fun we recently had together was when we:

....

....

Besides spending time with you, I really enjoy spending
time with .... because:

....

....

....

MOM

This is the actor who would play me in a movie of our lives:

....

This is the actress who would play you in a movie of our lives:

....

I love when you and I do ....
together because:

....

....

The most fun we recently had together was when we:

....

....

Besides spending time with you, I really enjoy spending
time with .... because:

....

....

....

SON

Who has inspired you lately to be more kind?

....

What did they do or say that motivated you?

....
....
....
....
....
....

Tell me about the nicest thing you've ever done for
someone else.

....
....
....
....
....
....
....

MOM

Who has inspired you lately to be more kind?

....

What did they do or say that motivated you?

....

....

....

....

....

....

Tell me about the nicest thing you've ever done for someone else.

....

....

....

....

....

....

....

SON

FREE WRITING SPACE

....

....

....

....

....

....

....

....

....

....

....

....

....

....

....

....

....

....

....

....

....

....

mom

FREE WRITING SPACE

....

....

....

....

....

....

....

....

....

....

....

....

....

....

....

....

....

....

SON

MONTH FIVE

....

If I were a superhero, my name would be:

....

My superpower would be:

....

The last time I tried something new, I:

....

....

I am proud of myself for:

....

....

....

This is something I wish I had done differently:

....

....

....

MOM

If I were a superhero, my name would be:

....

My superpower would be:

....

The last time I tried something new, I:

....

....

I am proud of myself for:

....

....

....

This is something I wish I had done differently:

....

....

....

SON

Make an anagram of your name.

....

Do you like your name? Why or why not? If not, what would
you want it to be?

....

....

....

....

....

....

Tell me the story of how you chose my name and why.

....

....

....

....

....

....

....

mom

Make an anagram of your name.

....

Do you like your name? Why or why not?

....

....

....

....

....

....

....

If you got to choose your own name, what would it be
and why?

....

....

....

....

....

....

....

SON

When you do this, it reminds me of myself because:

....
....
....
....
....
....
....
....

When I was younger, I wish I'd been ....
like you because:

....
....
....
....
....
....
....
....

mom

When you do this, it reminds me of myself because:

....

....

....

....

....

....

....

....

I hope I am .... like you when I'm older because:

....

....

....

....

....

....

....

....

SON

You're a wonderful son because:

....
....
....
....
....
....
....
....
....
....
....
....
....
....
....
....
....
....
....
....
....

mom

I like having you as my mother because:

....

....

....

....

....

....

....

....

....

....

....

....

....

....

....

....

....

....

....

SON

What's something you've done as a mother that you thought you'd never do?

....

....

....

....

What made you change your mind?

....

....

....

How do you feel about the change?

....

....

....

....

....

....

....

MOM

What's something you changed your mind about recently?

....
....
....
....

What made you change your mind?

....
....
....

How do you feel about the change?

....
....
....
....
....
....
....

SON

FREE WRITING SPACE

mom

FREE WRITING SPACE

....

....

....

....

....

....

....

....

....

....

....

....

....

....

....

....

....

....

....

SON

MONTH SIX

....

What's something that put you in a good mood this week?

....

....

....

What's something you're looking forward to?

....

....

....

....

For my next birthday, I want to celebrate by:

....

....

....

....

....

....

....

MOM

What's something that put you in a good mood this week?

....
....
....

What's something you're looking forward to?

....
....
....
....

For my next birthday, I want to celebrate by:

....
....
....
....
....
....
....
....

SON

What would your friends say if they were describing you to someone who didn't know you?

....

....

....

....

....

....

....

....

Share the most embarrassing thing that happened to you when you were a kid.

....

....

....

....

....

....

....

....

....

mom

What would your friends say if they were describing you to someone who didn't know you?

....

....

....

....

....

....

....

Tell me about a time when you were embarrassed in front of your friends.

....

....

....

....

....

....

....

....

SON

My favorite sight is .... because:

....

....

My favorite sound is .... because:

....

....

My favorite smell is .... because:

....

....

My favorite taste is .... because:

....

....

The one item I could never get rid of is ....

.... because:

....

....

mom

My favorite sight is .... because:

....

....

My favorite sound is .... because:

....

....

My favorite smell is .... because:

....

....

My favorite taste is .... because:

....

....

The one item I could never get rid of is ....

.... because:

....

....

SON

Do you prefer being around lots of people or having alone time? Why?

....
....
....
....
....
....
....

Do you find it easy or difficult to make friends? Why?

....
....
....
....
....
....
....
....

mom

Do you prefer being around lots of people or having alone time? Why?

....
....
....
....
....
....
....

Do you find it easy or difficult to make friends? Why?

....
....
....
....
....
....
....
....

SON

FREE WRITING SPACE

....
....
....
....
....
....
....
....
....
....
....
....
....
....
....
....
....
....
....
....

mom

FREE WRITING SPACE

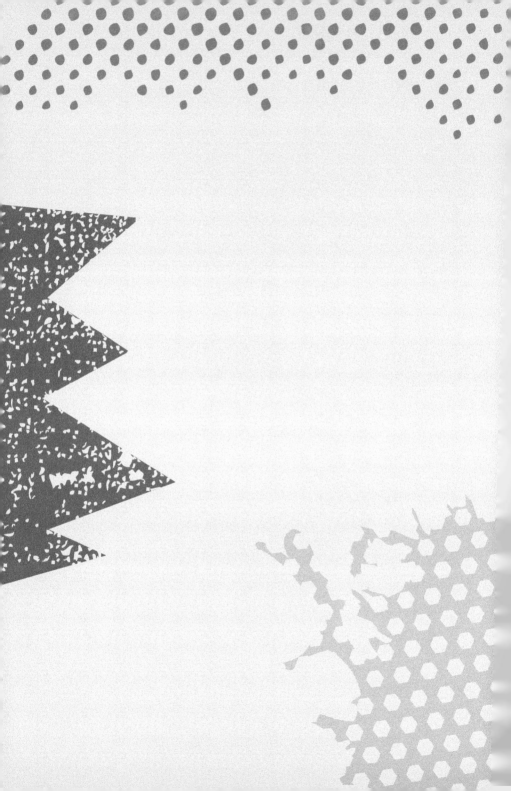

MONTH SEVEN

....

My best friends are ....
because:

....

....

....

These are the qualities I value in a friend:

....

....

....

....

....

....

These are the ways I want to be a better friend:

....

....

....

....

....

....

MOM

My best friends are ....
because:

....

....

....

These are the qualities I value in a friend:

....

....

....

....

....

....

These are the ways I want to be a better friend:

....

....

....

....

....

....

SON

When you were my age, who was your best friend?

....
....
....
....
....
....
....
....
....

My longest friendship is with ....,
and the reasons we've remained friends for so long are:

....
....
....
....
....
....
....
....

mom

How would you describe me to your friends?

....

....

....

....

....

....

....

....

My longest friendship is with ....,
and the reasons we've remained friends for so long are:

....

....

....

....

....

....

....

....

SON

These are some assumptions people have about me:

....
....
....
....
....

They make me feel:

....
....
....
....

I wish more people knew this fact about me:

....
....
....
....
....
....

mom

These are some assumptions people have about me:

....
....
....
....
....

They make me feel:

....
....
....
....

I wish more people knew this fact about me:

....
....
....
....
....
....

SON

The naughtiest thing I ever did was:

....

....

....

Why did you do it, and did you suffer any consequences? If
so, what?

....

....

....

....

....

....

....

....

....

....

....

....

....

MOM

The naughtiest thing I ever did was:

....
....
....

Why did you do it, and did you suffer any consequences? If so, what?

....
....
....
....
....
....
....
....
....
....
....
....
....

SON

What's something you wish you could get a second chance at, and why?

....

....

....

....

....

....

....

What would you do differently?

....

....

....

....

....

....

....

....

MOM

What's something you wish you could get a second chance at, and why?

....
....
....
....
....
....
....

What would you do differently?

....
....
....
....
....
....
....
....

SON

FREE WRITING SPACE

....
....
....
....
....
....
....
....
....
....
....
....
....
....
....
....
....
....
....
....

mom

FREE WRITING SPACE

SON

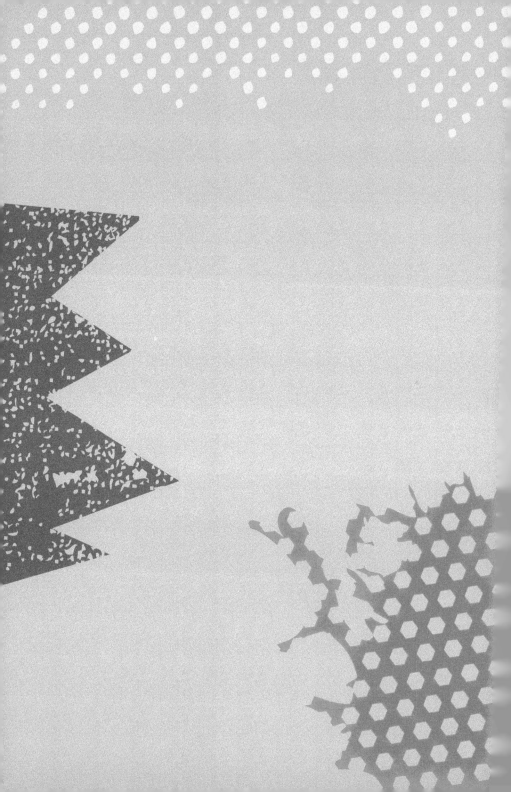

MONTH EIGHT

·························

My favorite tradition of ours is ....
because:

....

....

....

Do you think work and school get in the way of "us time"?
Why or why not?

....

....

....

Some suggestions I have for making more time for us are:

....

....

....

....

....

....

....

....

MOM

My favorite tradition of ours is .... because:

....

....

....

Do you think work and school get in the way of "us time"? Why or why not?

....

....

....

Some suggestions I have for making more time for us are:

....

....

....

....

....

....

....

....

SON

Sometimes you hurt my feelings when you do this:

....
....
....
....
....

Whenever we have a disagreement, I feel:

....
....
....
....

When we have an argument, this is my favorite way to make up:

....
....
....
....
....

MOM

Sometimes you hurt my feelings when you do this:

....

....

....

....

....

Whenever we have a disagreement, I feel:

....

....

....

....

When we have an argument, this is my favorite way to
make up:

....

....

....

....

....

SON

Tell me about a time you argued with someone close to you.
What caused the disagreement and how did you resolve it?

....

....

....

....

....

....

....

....

....

....

....

....

....

....

....

....

....

....

mom

Tell me about a time you argued with someone close to you. What caused the disagreement and how did you resolve it?

....

....

....

....

....

....

....

....

....

....

....

....

....

....

....

....

SON

If I were in charge of everybody, I would make these laws:

....

....

....

....

....

....

If you had a million dollars and had to spend it all in one day, what would you do?

....

....

....

....

....

....

....

....

....

....

....

MOM

If I were in charge of everybody, I would make these laws:

....

....

....

....

....

....

If you had a million dollars and had to spend it all in one day, what would you do?

....

....

....

....

....

....

....

....

....

....

....

SON

Tell me about someone in our family I don't know or don't know well.

....
....
....
....
....
....
....
....
....
....
....
....
....
....
....
....
....
....
....
....

mom

Tell me about a friend or teacher I don't know or don't know well.

....
....
....
....
....
....
....
....
....
....
....
....
....
....
....
....
....
....

SON

FREE WRITING SPACE

....
....
....
....
....
....
....
....
....
....
....
....
....
....
....
....
....
....
....
....
....

mom

FREE WRITING SPACE

....

....

....

....

....

....

....

....

....

....

....

....

....

....

....

....

....

....

SON

MONTH NINE

These are the books, TV shows, movies, and activities I
want to complete:

....

....

....

....

....

....

....

....

....

....

....

....

....

....

....

....

....

....

mom

These are the books, TV shows, movies, and activities I want to complete:

....

....

....

....

....

....

....

....

....

....

....

....

....

....

....

....

....

SON

Can mothers and sons be friends? Why or why not?

....

....

....

....

....

....

....

This is my response to what you wrote about mothers and
sons being friends:

....

....

....

....

....

....

....

mom

Can mothers and sons be friends? Why or why not?

....

....

....

....

....

....

....

This is my response to what you wrote about mothers and sons being friends:

....

....

....

....

....

....

....

....

SON

If I could be something other than a human, I'd be ....
.... because:

....

....

....

Do you ever wish you could switch places with me? Why or
why not?

....

....

....

....

....

If we did switch places, I'd do these things:

....

....

....

....

....

....

mom

If I could be something other than a human, I'd be .... because:

....

....

....

Do you ever wish you could switch places with me? Why or why not?

....

....

....

....

....

If we did switch places, I'd do these things:

....

....

....

....

....

....

SON

Ten things I'm grateful for right now:

1. ....
....

2. ....
....

3. ....
....

4. ....
....

5. ....
....

6. ....
....

7. ....
....

8. ....
....

9. ....
....

10. ....
....

mom

Ten things I'm grateful for right now:

1. ....
....

2. ....
....

3. ....
....

4. ....
....

5. ....
....

6. ....
....

7. ....
....

8. ....
....

9. ....
....

10. ....
....

SON

Tell me a story about your first romantic relationship.

....

....

....

....

....

....

....

....

What are some things you want me to know about dating
and falling in love?

....

....

....

....

....

....

....

....

mom

Do you and your friends talk about dating? What do you talk about? What do you want to know about dating and falling in love?

....

....

....

....

....

....

....

....

....

....

....

....

....

....

....

....

SON

FREE WRITING SPACE

....

....

....

....

....

....

....

....

....

....

....

....

....

....

....

....

....

mom

FREE WRITING SPACE

....

....

....

....

....

....

....

....

....

....

....

....

....

....

....

....

....

....

....

....

....

SON

MONTH TEN

••••••••••••••••••••••••••••••

If we were to host a talk show together, it would be called
...., and our theme song
would be:

....

....

Do you think I appreciate you? Why or why not?

....

....

What's something I could do to show my appreciation for
you more often?

....

....

....

The next time we have a day together, let's:

....

....

....

mom

If we were to host a talk show together, it would be called
...., and our theme song
would be:

....

....

Do you think I appreciate you? Why or why not?

....

....

What's something I could do to show my appreciation for
you more often?

....

....

....

The next time we have a day together, let's:

....

....

....

SON

If you were running for president, what would your platform be?

....

....

....

....

....

What's one social issue that's really important to you? Why do you care about it so much?

....

....

....

....

If there was one thing I could change right now about the world we live in, it would be:

....

....

....

....

MOM

If you were running for president, what would you promise your voters?

....

....

....

....

....

What's one social issue that's really important to you? Why do you care about it so much?

....

....

....

....

If there was one thing I could change right now about the world we live in, it would be:

....

....

....

....

SON

What's the best advice you ever received, and who shared it
with you?

....
....
....
....
....
....
....
....

How have you put that advice into practice?

....
....
....
....
....
....
....
....

mom

What's the best advice you ever received, and who shared it with you?

....
....
....
....
....
....
....
....

How have you put that advice into practice?

....
....
....
....
....
....
....
....

SON

What's one dream goal you want to accomplish?

....
....
....
....
....
....
....
....

How would you accomplish this goal?

....
....
....
....
....
....
....
....

MOM

What's one dream goal you want to accomplish?

....
....
....
....
....
....
....
....

How would you accomplish this goal?

....
....
....
....
....
....
....
....
....

SON

If you could go back in time and tell your past self anything, what would it be and why?

....
....
....
....
....
....
....
....
....
....
....
....
....
....
....
....
....
....
....
....
....

MOM

What lesson have you recently learned that you think will really help you in the future as an adult, and why?

....

....

....

....

....

....

....

....

....

....

....

....

....

....

....

....

....

SON

FREE WRITING SPACE

....

....

....

....

....

....

....

....

....

....

....

....

....

....

....

....

....

....

....

mom

FREE WRITING SPACE

....
....
....
....
....
....
....
....
....
....
....
....
....
....
....
....
....
....
....
....

SON

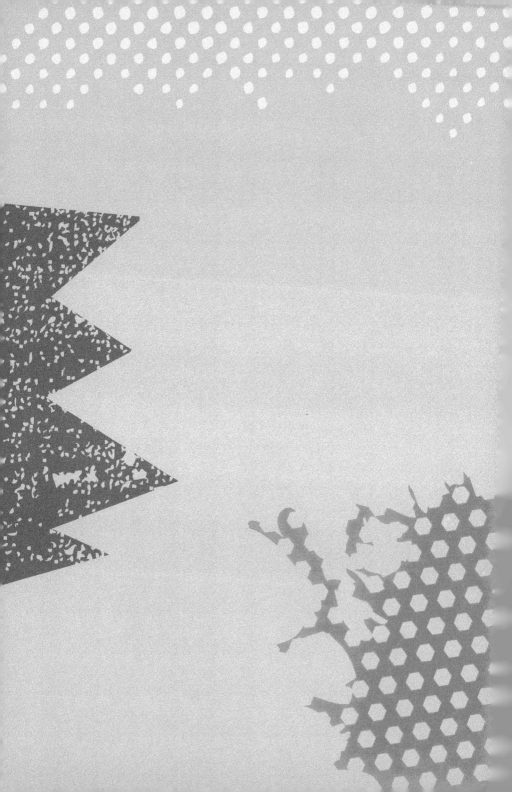

MONTH ELEVEN

If I had to live on a deserted island, these are four things I'd bring:

1. ....
2. ....
3. ....
4. ....

If I could only eat three foods for the rest of my life, they would be:

1. ....
2. ....
3. ....

If I could try four careers for fun, they would be:

1. ....
2. ....
3. ....
4. ....

MOM

If I had to live on a deserted island, these are four things I'd bring:

1. ....

2. ....

3. ....

4. ....

If I could only eat three foods for the rest of my life, they would be:

1. ....

2. ....

3. ....

If I could try four careers for fun, they would be:

1. ....

2. ....

3. ....

4. ....

SON

Tell me about a time when you were wrong about something. What was the situation? How did you handle it? What did you do when you realized you were wrong?

....

....

....

....

....

....

....

....

....

....

....

....

....

....

....

....

....

....

....

MOM

Tell me about a time when you didn't handle a problem well. What happened? What would you do differently?

....

....

....

....

....

....

....

....

....

....

....

....

....

....

....

....

SON

The title of my autobiography would be:

....

The celebrity I would change places with is:

....

My favorite age I've been so far is .... because:

....

....

The best gift I ever received was ....
because:

....

....

....

....

....

....

MOM

The title of my autobiography would be:

....

The celebrity I would change places with is:

....

My favorite age I've been so far is .... because:

....

....

....

The best gift I ever received was ....
because:

....

....

....

....

....

....

....

SON

What's something you've learned from me but never
told me?

....

....

....

....

....

....

....

This is what I've learned from you:

....

....

....

....

....

....

....

....

MOM

What's something you've learned from me but never
told me?

....
....
....
....
....
....
....
....

This is what I've learned from you:

....
....
....
....
....
....
....
....

SON

Tell me about the most magical or unexpected experience you've ever had.

....
....
....
....
....
....
....
....
....
....
....
....
....
....
....
....
....
....

MOM

Tell me about the most magical or unexpected experience you've ever had.

....
....
....
....
....
....
....
....
....
....
....
....
....
....
....
....
....
....

SON

FREE WRITING SPACE

FREE WRITING SPACE

....

....

....

....

....

....

....

....

....

....

....

....

....

....

....

....

....

SON

MONTH TWELVE

If you could see into your future, would you want to? Why or why not?

....
....
....
....
....

If a genie appeared and granted you three wishes, what would they be?

....
....
....
....

If you could speak to someone who has died, who would it be, and what would you talk to them about?

....
....
....
....

mom

If you could see into your future, would you want to? Why or why not?

....

....

....

....

....

If a genie appeared and granted you three wishes, what would they be?

....

....

....

....

If you could speak to someone who has died, who would it be, and what would you talk to them about?

....

....

....

....

SON

If you could choose to be super smart or super popular,
which would you choose, and why?

....

....

....

....

....

....

....

....

....

....

....

....

....

....

....

....

....

....

mom

If you could choose to be super smart or super popular, which would you choose, and why?

....

....

....

....

....

....

....

....

....

....

....

....

....

....

....

....

....

SON

Tell me about a time when you had to be a leader. What was the situation? Who did you have to lead? Did people listen to you? What did you learn about leadership?

....

....

....

....

....

....

....

....

....

....

....

....

....

....

....

....

....

MOM

Tell me about a time when you had to be in charge. Did you like being in that role? Did people accept you as a leader? What did that experience teach you about leadership?

....

....

....

....

....

....

....

....

....

....

....

....

....

....

....

....

SON

I feel insecure about .... because:

....

....

....

....

....

The last time I cried was .... because:

....

....

....

....

....

The last time I was angry was .... because:

....

....

....

....

....

mom

I feel insecure about .... because:

....

....

....

....

....

The last time I cried was .... because:

....

....

....

....

....

The last time I was angry was .... because:

....

....

....

....

....

SON

What I love most about where I grew up:

....
....
....
....
....
....
....

If I could go anywhere in the world, it would be:

....
....
....
....
....
....
....
....

MOM

What I love most about where I grew up:

....
....
....
....
....
....
....
....

If I could go anywhere in the world, it would be:

....
....
....
....
....
....
....
....

SON

FREE WRITING SPACE

....

....

....

....

....

....

....

....

....

....

....

....

....

....

....

....

....

mom

FREE WRITING SPACE

....
....
....
....
....
....
....
....
....
....
....
....
....
....
....
....
....
....
....
....
....
....
....
....
....

SON

REFLECTING ON
THE YEAR

Well done! It's the end of your year of journaling together. Even though you may have had tough conversations, you also spent the last 12 months sharing laughs and learning so much more about each other than you knew before.

What do you do now that your journal is complete? Keep asking questions. Continue to be curious about each other. Talk. Listen.

It's awesome having a special person in your life who cares enough about you to want to know your likes, dislikes, dreams, and hopes, and share her own. Never forget what a gift that is.

WE FINISHED THIS JOURNAL TOGETHER ON

A PICTURE OR PHOTO OF US AT THE END OF THE YEAR

1. Before we started, how did we feel about doing this journal together?

....

....

....

....

....

2. What is our favorite part about having completed this journal together?

....

....

....

....

....

3. What's the most surprising thing we've learned about each other?

....

....

....

....

....

4. How have we personally changed through journaling together?

....

....

....

....

....

5. How is our relationship different now?

....

....

....

....

....

6. What project would we like to do together next, and when should
   we begin?

....

....

....

....

CPSIA information can be obtained
at www.ICGtesting.com
Printed in the USA
JSHW050923071221
21039JS00001B/1